A Guide to
AMERICAN STATES

Missouri

THE SHOW ME STATE

MEDIA ENHANCED BOOKS

AV²
BY WEIGL

ADDED VALUE • AUDIO VISUAL

www.av2books.com

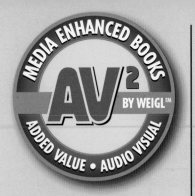

AV² provides enriched content that supplements and complements this book Weigl's AV² books strive to create inspired learning and engage young mind in a total learning experience.

Your AV² Media Enhanced books come alive with...

Go to **www.av2books.com**, and enter this book's unique code.

BOOK CODE

C 7 8 4 9 1 2

AV² by Weigl brings you media enhanced books that support active learning.

Audio
Listen to sections of the book read aloud.

Video
Watch informative video clips.

Embedded Weblinks
Gain additional information for research.

Try This!
Complete activities and hands-on experiments.

Key Words
Study vocabulary, and complete a matching word activity.

Quizzes
Test your knowledge.

Slide Show
View images and captions, and prepare a presentation.

... and much, much more

Published by AV² by Weigl
350 5th Avenue, 59th Floor
New York, NY 10118
Website: www.av2books.com   www.weigl.com

Library of Congress Cataloging-in-Publication Data

Evdokimoff, Natasha.
 Missouri / Natasha Evdokimoff.
    p. cm. -- (A guide to American states)
 Includes index.
 ISBN 978-1-61690-797-6 (hardcover : alk. paper) -- ISBN 978-1-61690-473-9 (online)
 1. Missouri--Juvenile literature. I. Title.
 F466.3.E945 2011
 977.8--dc23
                              2011018337

Printed in the United States of America in North Mankato, Minnesota

052011
WEP180511

Project Coordinator Jordan McGill
Art Director Terry Paulhus

Photo Credits
Every reasonable effort has been made to trace ownership and to obtain permission to reprint copyright material. The publishers would be pleased to have any errors or omissions brought to their attention so that they may be corrected in subsequent printings.

Weigl acknowledges Getty Images as its primary image supplier for this title.

Contents

Nearly 30 million acres of land in Missouri is used as farmland. Farm products bring almost $4 billion a year into Missouri's economy.

Introduction

Missouri gets its name from the river that flows through it. The river is named for a group of American Indians and may mean "people having canoes." Today Missouri is known as the Show Me State. The nickname probably came from Congressman Willard Vandiver, who said in 1899, "I am from Missouri, you have got to show me." In other words, the people of his state are not impressed by fancy speechmaking. For them, actions speak louder than words.

Missouri was the starting point for many journeys westward. In 1804 the explorers Meriwether Lewis and William Clark began their voyage of discovery from near St. Louis. The Lewis and Clark Expedition led the way for American trade and settlement in the West.

The Missouri River drains nearly one-sixth of the area of the United States. At about 2,300 miles, it is one of the longest rivers in the United States.

The area of 18th and Vine Streets in Kansas City is known for the birth of several forms of jazz in the early 20th century. Today the area is the home of the Blue Room, a jazz club named after the 1930s club where jazz legends such as Charlie Parker played.

Until 1845 Missouri was the nation's westernmost state and was known as the Gateway to the West. Many pioneers traveled through Missouri on their way to California, Oregon, and other areas in the West.

In the 20th century Missouri was a place of cultural innovation. In the 1920s, St. Louis and Kansas City made important contributions to both jazz and blues music. "The St. Louis Blues" is one of the best-known blues songs of all time. In the second half of the 20th century, Missouri's schools struggled with racial **segregation**. Today changes to the educational system are helping Missourians look to a bright future.

Where Is Missouri?

In Missouri, the eastern forests meet the western prairies. North of the Missouri River are gently rolling hills and **fertile** plains. Much of the land south of the river lies in the Ozark Mountains. In the southeastern part of the state, there is a low-lying plain that drains into the Mississippi River.

Cattle ranches cover much of the land in western Missouri. Missouri ranks ninth in the United States in the value of sales of cattle and calves.

Missouri has characteristics of several regions of the United States. Its cornfields are reminders of the Midwest, while its cotton fields reflect the South. Missouri's cattle ranches are a fond reminder of the West, and the state's factories recall those found in the East. In politics, Missouri is often referred to as a "swing state," and it often votes for the winner in presidential elections.

The Missouri River flows from west to east across the state. It connects Kansas City in the west to the capital of Jefferson City in the central part of the state. Then it flows from Jefferson City to St. Louis, on the state's eastern border.

The **confluence** of the Mississippi and Missouri rivers, near St. Louis, has been a crossroads of North America since American Indians ruled the land. Rivers brought European explorers, settlers, and traders into the region. Today Missouri also has nearly 125,000 miles of public roads binding the state together. Missouri also has many airports to serve air travelers. St. Louis and Kansas City have the state's main public airports. Missouri is also a rail center, crisscrossed by many miles of tracks. Passenger trains run between St. Louis and Kansas City.

I DIDN'T KNOW THAT!

Missouri Day is held every year on the third Wednesday in October. It is a day for people to celebrate the achievements of Missourians.

Kansas City calls itself the Heart of America because it is not far from the geographic center of the 48 contiguous states. These are the states that are all connected to one another.

The Gateway Arch provides St. Louis with a unique skyline.

The Santa Fe and the Oregon trails both started at Independence. Westward-bound settlers and traders followed these trails before railroads were built.

The Mississippi River forms the eastern border of Missouri. The river allows easy transportation of goods, as it has for hundreds of years.

Mapping Missouri

N o state shares more borders with other states than Missouri. Arkansas is to the south, and Oklahoma, Kansas, and Nebraska are to the west. Iowa is to the north, and to the east, across the Mississippi River, are Illinois, Kentucky, and Tennessee.

Sites and Symbols

STATE SEAL
Missouri

STATE BIRD
Bluebird

STATE FLOWER
White Hawthorn

STATE FLAG
Missouri

STATE ANIMAL
Missouri Mule

STATE TREE
Flowering Dogwood

Nickname The Show Me State

Motto *Salus Populi Suprema Lex Esto* (Let the welfare of the people be the supreme law)

Song "Missouri Waltz," words by J. R. Shannon, music by John Valentine Eppel, and arrangement by Frederick Knight Logan

Entered the Union August 10, 1821, as the 24th state

Capital Jefferson City

Population (2010 Census) 5,988,927 Ranked 18th state

Map Labels

IOWA

Leon · Lamoni · Monmouth · Bloomfield · Fort Madison · Burlington · Peoria · Pontiac · 74

Tarkio · Maryville · Albany · Bethany · Unionville · Kirksville · Memphis · Keokuk · Bloomington

NE* · Savannah · Chillicothe · Marceline · Macon · Shelbina · Hannibal · Springfield · Decatur · Lincoln · 72

St. Joseph · Atchison · Pittsfield · Jacksonville

Platte City · Excelsior Springs · Moberly · Bowling Green · **ILLINOIS**

Leavenworth · Kansas City · Marshall · Mexico · Staunton · Vandalia · 70

Topeka · **Kansas City** · Boonville · **Columbia** · Florissant · Edwardsville · 57

Lawrence · **Overland Park** · Warrensburg · Sedalia · Fulton · **St. Louis** · **East St. Louis** · Salem

Ottawa · **MISSOURI** · **Jefferson City** · Union · 64 · 55

Garnett · Butler · Owensville · Sullivan · Festus · Mount Vernon

KANSAS · Iola · Nevada · Cuba · 44 · Rolla · Flat River · Benton · Herrin · Humboldt · Waynesville · Marion

Chanute · Lamar · Lebanon · Fredericktown

Parsons · Marshfield · Houston · Jackson · Cape Girardeau · 24

Coffeyville · Carthage · **Springfield** · Cabool · Sikeston · **KENTUCKY**

Miami · Joplin · Aurora · Monett · Ozark · New Madrid · Union City · Martin

Neosho · West Plains · Poplar Bluff · Malden · Dyersburg · Humboldt

OKLAHOMA · Bella Vista · Branson · Thayer · Corning · Kennett · Hayti

Claremore · Rogers · Mountain Home · Paragould · Blytheville · **TENNESSEE**

Fayetteville · Harrison · Hoxie

Tahlequah · **ARKANSAS** · Jonesboro · Trumann · 40

Muskogee · Newport

*Nebraska

LEGEND

— Road
— River
⭐ State Capital
• City
▨ Missouri
— State Border

N

Map Scale
0   100 Miles

STATE CAPITAL

Jefferson City was founded when Missouri became a state. It was named after Thomas Jefferson and was planned by Daniel M. Boone, son of the famed frontiersman Daniel Boone. Today more than 40,000 people make Jefferson City their home.

United States

Hawai'i · Alaska

Missouri

The Land

Missouri's landscape is a combination of rolling hills, deep valleys, lush forests, and flat farmland. Missouri's most important natural regions are the Central Lowland in the north, the Ozark Plateau in the south, and the Gulf Coastal Plain in the southeast.

There are some worn-down mountains in the south that rise no higher than 1,772 feet above sea level. Though not high compared to other ranges, they create a beautiful contrast to the rest of the state. The New Madrid Fault in the southeast produced severe earthquakes in 1811 and 1812. A fault is a deep crack in Earth's surface, and many earthquakes around the world occur at faults.

MISSISSIPPI RIVER

The Mississippi is the largest river in North America. It begins in Minnesota, emptying into the Gulf of Mexico about 2,340 miles later. As the Mississippi flows south past Missouri, both the Missouri and the Ohio rivers flow into it, making it very wide.

FORESTS

Forests grow in the hills south of the Missouri River. Missouri has more than 14 million acres of forest land, including 70 different kinds of trees and shrubs.

ONANDAGA CAVE

Missouri boasts more than 6,300 caves. Most of these are found in the Ozark Mountains, south of the Missouri River. Onandaga Cave in Leasburg has been the site of a state park since 1982.

RICH FARMLAND

Northern Missouri has rich soil and good drainage into rivers. These conditions make for excellent farmland.

Ha Ha Tonka State Park is a geological wonder, with sinkholes, caves, and distinct rock formations.

Missouri's largest lakes were made by damming streams and rivers. Most of these lakes were made to prevent flooding and create hydroelectric power. But they also act as recreational resources for the state.

The extreme southeast portion of Missouri is called the Bootheel because that is what it looks like on a map.

Missouri lies in "Tornado Alley," a region of the country where many tornadoes occur. Missouri experiences about 25 tornadoes a year.

Climate

The weather in Missouri is highly changeable. Temperatures often top 100° Fahrenheit in summer heat waves, and winter can bring low temperatures below 0° F. In winter the northwest is quite a bit colder than the southeast, but summer temperatures are about the same throughout the state. Summer humidity is high, and summer rain comes mostly in the form of drenching thunderstorms. Tornadoes occur as well in spring and summer.

Precipitation ranges from 34 inches per year in the northwest to 50 inches in the southeast. In the winter, the northern parts of the state receive the most snow.

Average Annual Precipitation Across Missouri

There can be great variation in precipitation among different cities in Missouri. How does location affect the amount of rainfall a city receives?

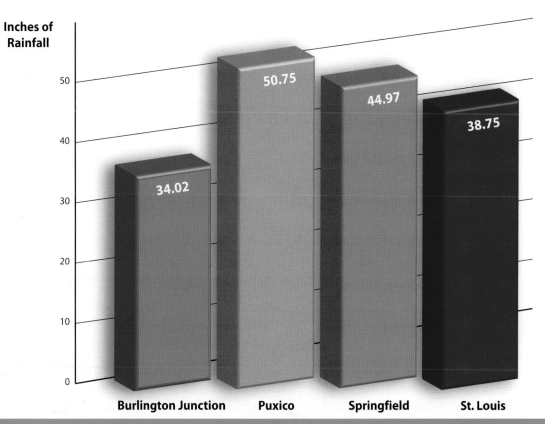

Inches of Rainfall

City	Inches
Burlington Junction	34.02
Puxico	50.75
Springfield	44.97
St. Louis	38.75

Natural Resources

Trees cover nearly one-third of Missouri. Oak, walnut, and red cedar trees are found across the state. Forestry is an important business in the state, with lumber, flooring, and railroad ties as the key wood products.

Lead deposits can be found in the New Lead Belt in southeastern Missouri. Missouri has led all other states in lead production for more than 75 years.

The state is also rich in minerals. Missouri has some of the world's largest deposits of lead. Lime, coal, barite, zinc, and iron ore are also mined. Missouri is a leading state in zinc and lime production. Minerals mined in Missouri are sold across the country. Other resources are found in smaller quantities.

The Bollinger Mill State Historic Site in Burfordville represents almost 200 years of milling history. There visitors can observe corn being ground by waterpower.

Missouri clay makes excellent bricks, and houses in St. Louis typically have brick construction.

Lead deposits near the Ozark National Scenic Riverways are not allowed to be developed, for environmental reasons.

The St. Francois Mountains are more than 1 billion years old and are known for their lead mines.

Missouri's mineral products include portland cement and crushed stone.

Mozarkite was named the official state rock on July 21, 1967.

Plants

Spring is a welcome time in Missouri. Some flowers, such as the spring beauty, bloom as early as the end of February. More than 3,200 species of plants, both native and introduced, grow in Missouri. Among native plants are the Missouri evening primrose, the cream wild indigo, and the Missouri coneflower. Flowers common to the state include violets, buttercups, and wild roses. Many types of wildflowers line Missouri's roadsides, including Queen Anne's lace, black-eyed Susan, blazing star, and wild sweet William. Wild grape, ivy, and honeysuckle are three of the state's leafy vines. Bluegrass can be found throughout Missouri, though it is not native to the area.

In the 1700s, around one-third of Missouri was covered in prairie grasses. Now almost all of the land that was once prairie is used as farmland. There are still a number of prairie reserves around the state, however.

WILD COLUMBINE

Wild columbine bloom in April and can grow as high as 2 feet. Flowers can be pink, purple, white, yellow, or red. They grow in a variety of soil conditions. They like shade but can also thrive in full sun.

MOCKERNUT HICKORY

The mockernut hickory is the most common variety of hickory tree. It can live as long as 500 years. Hickory is a hard wood, commonly growing in eastern forests.

VIOLETS

Violets are hardy plants that bloom in early spring. They are commonly found in the Ozark Mountains.

FLOWERING DOGWOOD

The flowering dogwood, Missouri's state tree, rarely grows over 40 feet. It is known for its tiny flowers of four pink or white petals.

Animals

About 70 species of mammals live in Missouri's forests and hills. Smaller mammals in the state include rabbits, woodchucks, minks, and opossums. Larger mammals include white-tailed deer, beavers, and coyotes. Black bears and even mountain lions can occasionally be found. Because of hunting and loss of their natural habitats, some species of animals have disappeared from Missouri. These include the gray wolf, the red wolf, the white-tailed jackrabbit, the Ozark big-eared bat, the elk, and the bison, or buffalo.

For bird-watchers, Missouri is an ideal location. Robins, bluebirds, cardinals, doves, and hawks grace the sky. Bass, pike, perch, and catfish provide good fishing in state waters. Hikers should be careful of poisonous rattlesnakes and copperhead snakes that are found in the hills.

FRANKLIN'S GROUND SQUIRREL

The Franklin's ground squirrel likes to live in tall grass or mid-grass prairies. It makes its nest in underground burrows. Since its habitat is disappearing, the ground squirrel population is decreasing.

EASTERN COTTONTAIL RABBIT

Eastern cottontail rabbits live in many areas of Missouri. They have brownish-red coats, slender faces, and a splash of white on the tail. They need good protective cover to survive in the wild.

WHITE-TAILED DEER

By 1890 the white-tailed deer was nearly extinct in Missouri. In 1944 deer populations were reported to have increased to about 15,000 because of conservation programs. White-tailed deer are now common throughout Missouri.

CHANNEL CATFISH

The channel catfish is Missouri's state fish. Although these fish can grow to 45 pounds, this is uncommon in Missouri. Channel catfish are bottom feeders, eating insects, mollusks, other fish, and plants.

I DIDN'T KNOW THAT!

The Missouri Department of Conservation works to protect and conserve the state's wildlife and natural resources. Every month the department holds events to educate the public about dangers to the environment and what they can do to help.

Black bears once roamed the state's forests in large numbers, but they were hunted to near **extinction** for their fur. The Missouri Department of Conservation is conducting a multi-year study to find out to what degree the black bear population has rebounded.

Missouri has supplied wild turkeys to Wisconsin and other states for release in successful reintroduction programs.

Missouri's owl population is in decline as a result of pollution and the disappearance of their habitat.

Tourism

Missouri's outdoors are a popular destination for vacationers from across the country. The scenic Ozark Mountains are found in the southern part of the state and are shared mostly with Arkansas. The Ozarks offer canyons, caves, and lush forests. The Bagnell Dam on the Osage River has created the Lake of the Ozarks. The lake is the largest **reservoir** in the state. It stretches for 92 miles from one end to the other. Golfing and camping are popular lakeside activities.

The Gateway Arch in St. Louis is another popular tourist attraction. The arch is a symbol of the city's role as the Gateway to the West. Every year more than 1 million people visit this structure. It is the tallest national monument in the country.

GATEWAY ARCH

At 630 feet, the Gateway Arch is more than twice as tall as the Statue of Liberty. It is as wide at its base as it is high. The arch is located on the Mississippi River. Visitors can ride to the top to enjoy spectacular views.

JOHNSON'S SHUT-INS STATE PARK

Johnson's Shut-Ins State Park is located on the shore of the Taum Sauk Reservoir. A boardwalk provides access to the shut-ins, which are narrow canyons in a wide valley.

LAKE OF THE OZARKS

More than 3 million people visit the Lake of the Ozarks each year. It is the largest lake in Missouri. The lake is a popular destination for wake boarders, water-skiers, swimmers, and boaters.

HANNIBAL

Readers of American literature will want to visit Hannibal, the author Samuel Clemens's boyhood home. Visitors can cruise the Mississippi on the Mark Twain Riverboat. During Tom Sawyer Days in July, people enjoy frog jumping contests, mud volleyball, and the National Fence Painting Contest.

Jesse James, the well-known bandit of the Old West, was born in Missouri in 1847. People can visit the home where he died in St. Joseph.

The Climatron Conservatory, in St. Louis, is a 70-foot-tall **geodesic dome** that shelters tropical plants all year. The Climatron was designed by architect R. Buckminster Fuller and was completed in 1960.

Branson is known as the Live Theater Capital of the World.

Industry

Missouri is known as a manufacturing state. More than $30 billion is earned through the sale of manufactured goods every year. Transportation equipment, including cars, trucks, and airplanes, is manufactured in the state. Missouri also has a food-processing industry that produces soft drinks, flour, meats, and canned fruits. Other Missouri-made products include soaps, detergents, missiles, and chemicals for farming and for medicines.

Industries in Missouri
Value of Goods and Services in Millions of Dollars

Many different industries are important in the state. What evidence allows you to conclude that Missouri's economy is well-balanced?

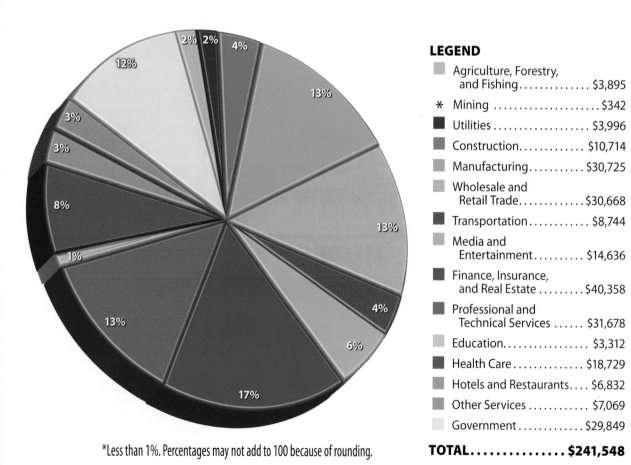

LEGEND

Agriculture, Forestry, and Fishing	$3,895
* Mining	$342
Utilities	$3,996
Construction	$10,714
Manufacturing	$30,725
Wholesale and Retail Trade	$30,668
Transportation	$8,744
Media and Entertainment	$14,636
Finance, Insurance, and Real Estate	$40,358
Professional and Technical Services	$31,678
Education	$3,312
Health Care	$18,729
Hotels and Restaurants	$6,832
Other Services	$7,069
Government	$29,849
TOTAL	**$241,548**

*Less than 1%. Percentages may not add to 100 because of rounding.

Kansas City and St. Louis are the major manufacturing centers in Missouri. Kansas City's location near the Great Plains makes it a perfect place for businesses that process agricultural products. In St. Louis the industries are mostly mechanical. Automobile assembly and aerospace technology make St. Louis a high-technology center. Anheuser-Busch, based in St. Louis, is one of the world's largest brewers. The company operates 12 breweries across the United States.

Producing cars, trucks, and other transportation equipment accounts for more than 16 percent of all manufacturing in Missouri. Recently, electric vehicles have become part of this production.

Missouri has about 100 wineries. Missouri's grape and wine industry is nearly 150 years old. The state's wineries attract more than 2.5 million visitors each year.

Every Chevrolet Corvette from 1954 to 1981 was made in St. Louis.

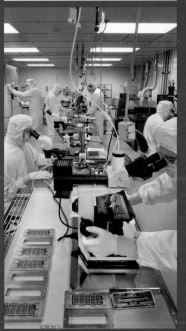

Missouri's top five exports are transportation equipment, chemicals, machinery, food and food products, and computer and electronic products. The areas where computer chips are manufactured are called clean rooms. They must be free of all germs.

Missouri has the fourth most diversified economy in the nation.

Goods and Services

There are more than 100,000 farms in Missouri. Farms in Missouri produce a variety of goods. The state is one of the country's leading producers of hay. Other important crops include corn, oats, rice, and tobacco. Much of the state's corn and hay crops are used to feed livestock. Cotton, rice, soybeans, sorghum, and wheat grow especially well in southeast Missouri. Soybeans are the state's most valuable crop. In recent years, about 5 million acres of land have been planted with soybeans in Missouri.

In most of the south the land is too rugged for crops, but it is suitable for raising livestock. The sale of animals and animal products contributes almost $3 billion to Missouri's economy each year. Large livestock farms raise cows and hogs. In some areas cows and hogs outnumber people. At other farms chickens are raised for their meat and eggs. Milk is produced at dairy farms, which are most commonly found in southwestern Missouri.

Soybeans are an important crop in Missouri. A farmer near Purdy set a world record in 2010 for the number of bushels of soybean grown per acre. The farmer grew 160.6 bushels per acre.

Transportation and aerospace equipment is also produced in the state. The McDonnell Douglas Corporation was known as a major producer of military aircraft and space vehicles. The company's history in Missouri dates back to 1939, when McDonnell Aircraft was founded. McDonnell Douglas was Missouri's largest private employer for many years. In 1997 the company was purchased by the Boeing Company.

The service sector also contributes greatly to the state's economy. More people work in service jobs than in any other type of employment. Service employees in Missouri work in hotels, restaurants, and stores, among many other places. There are almost 2.7 million nonfarm employees in Missouri. Trade, transportation, and utilities employ about 517,000 people, while manufacturing employs only around 203,000.

More than 200,000 Missourians work in hotels and restaurants.

American Indians

The first American Indians in the Missouri area may have roamed the land as early as 12,000 years ago, hunting big game animals, but little is known about them. More than 2,000 years ago came the Woodland culture, whose people raised corn, beans, and squash and made pottery.

In about 800 AD the Mound Builders of the Mississippian culture arrived. These people farmed, lived in villages, and were ruled by chiefs who made their headquarters atop large earthen mounds. It is believed that these mounds also served as burial sites and places of worship.

The Monks Mound, built by the Mound Builder people, is the largest human-made earthen mound in North America. It is located just across the Mississippi River from St. Louis.

By the 1600s, a number of American Indian groups lived in what is now Missouri. The Osage, the Crow, the Blackfoot, and the Sioux had settled in villages in the western part of the state. In the east were the Missouri and the Iowa tribes. The area contained bison and other wild animals that were hunted for food. Fish were plentiful in the nearby rivers. Animal skins were used for shelter and clothing. Some American Indian groups farmed Missouri's fertile land.

By the 1830s most of Missouri's native peoples had been driven out of the state by European settlement. Many of them were moved to **reservations** in what is now Oklahoma.

The Osage people spoke a Siouan language. They occupied a large area between the Missouri and the Arkansas rivers.

St. Louis was formerly called the Mound City for its many Indian mounds. The mounds were cleared away many years ago.

Missouri's American Indians lived almost half of the year in settled villages. The remainder of the year was spent on the move, hunting game.

In the 1600s the Osage first encountered French explorers near the Osage River, in what is now Missouri. The Osage were the largest group of American Indians in the Missouri area.

Once the crops were planted near their villages, the Osage went on long hunting trips, which lasted most of the spring and summer.

The Missouri History Museum in St. Louis presents exhibits of American Indian life in Missouri before European exploration.

In 1673, French explorers Father Jacques Marquette and Louis Jolliet charted the Mississippi River by canoe, accompanied by American Indian guides. They set foot on land that would later become Missouri.

Explorers and Missionaries

The first Europeans to see Missouri were two French explorers, Louis Jolliet and Father Jacques Marquette, who voyaged down the Mississippi River in 1673. In 1682 the entire Mississippi River **drainage basin**, including Missouri, was claimed for France by René-Robert Cavelier, sieur de La Salle.

In the years following La Salle's voyage, French fur trappers, fur traders, and missionaries moved into the Missouri region. In 1700 the Mission of St. Francis Xavier was established near the site of St. Louis, but it lasted only three years because it had been built on swampy ground. Not long afterward the French found the Missouri hills to the south to be a valuable source of lead, which they used to make ammunition. However, it was not until about 1735 that Missouri got its first permanent European settlement, at Ste. Genevieve.

Timeline of Settlement

Early Exploration

1673 Louis Jolliet and Father Jacques Marquette voyage down Mississippi River.

1682 René-Robert Cavelier, sieur de La Salle, claims Missouri for France.

European Settlements

1700 The Mission of St. Francis Xavier is established near the site of St. Louis.

1735 Ste. Genevieve, the first permanent European settlement in Missouri, is founded.

1764 St. Louis is founded as a fur-trading post near the confluence of the Missouri and Mississippi rivers.

U.S. Territory

1803 The United States purchases the Louisiana Territory, including Missouri, from France.

1804 The Lewis and Clark Expedition to explore the Louisiana Territory starts in Missouri.

Road to Statehood

1812 The U.S. government establishes the Missouri Territory.

1820 Senator Henry Clay of Kentucky proposes the Missouri Compromise, which allows Missouri to enter the Union as a slaveholding state.

1821 Missouri becomes the 24th state.

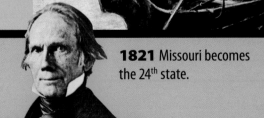

Early Settlers

I n 1764 a French fur-trading party led by Pierre Laclède set up a trading post on the west bank of the Mississippi River, just south of where the Missouri flows into it. Only a few months later the party learned that its new village, which was called St. Louis, sat on territory that France had transferred to Spain. The Spanish made St. Louis the capital of Upper Louisiana.

Map of Settlements and Resources in Early Missouri

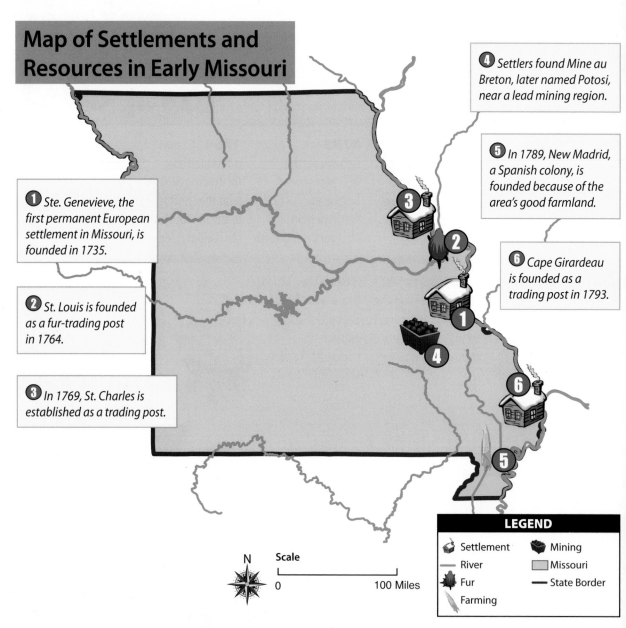

4 Settlers found Mine au Breton, later named Potosi, near a lead mining region.

5 In 1789, New Madrid, a Spanish colony, is founded because of the area's good farmland.

1 Ste. Genevieve, the first permanent European settlement in Missouri, is founded in 1735.

6 Cape Girardeau is founded as a trading post in 1793.

2 St. Louis is founded as a fur-trading post in 1764.

3 In 1769, St. Charles is established as a trading post.

N

Scale

0   100 Miles

LEGEND

🏠	Settlement	⛏️	Mining
—	River		Missouri
🍁	Fur	—	State Border
🌽	Farming		

Spain returned control of the Louisiana Territory to France in 1800, and in 1803 the United States purchased the land. The Lewis and Clark Expedition to explore the territory started out from a base near St. Louis in 1804. By that year more than 10,000 people were living in Missouri. In the second decade of the 1800s steamboats began to navigate on the Mississippi River, making travel and immigration much easier. In 1812 Missouri was organized into a territory by the U.S. government.

The French and the Spanish had allowed slavery in Missouri, and the Americans continued the practice. This caused problems in 1818, when Missouri applied to join the Union as a state. The Union was evenly divided between **free states** and **slave states**. Missouri had to wait until a free state, Maine, had been admitted before gaining statehood itself in 1821. The agreement that allowed Maine and Missouri to be admitted was called the Missouri Compromise.

Even though slavery was allowed in Missouri, most residents did not want the state to be a part of the **Confederacy** when the Civil War erupted in 1861. Like several other slaveholding states along the border between the North and the South, Missouri stayed in the Union.

Steamboat traffic grew rapidly with westward expansion. The construction of steamboats in St. Louis began in the mid-1800s.

Notable People

Many notable Missourians have contributed to the development of their state and their country. One even became president of the United States. Other Missourians were political leaders, began a huge chain of retail stores, made scientific discoveries, and wrote literature that has defined the American experience.

THOMAS HART BENTON (1782–1858)

Born in North Carolina, Thomas Hart Benton settled in St. Louis in 1815. He served Missouri as a U. S. senator from 1821 to 1851. Benton was a tireless supporter of western expansion and farming interests while in the Senate.

SAMUEL CLEMENS (MARK TWAIN) (1835–1910)

Samuel Clemens was born in Florida, Missouri, and grew up in Hannibal. He took the pen name Mark Twain and became one of the most popular writers in American literature. Clemens used his boyhood memories as material for some of his best-known novels, *Adventures of Tom Sawyer* and *The Adventures of Huckleberry Finn*. His humor, his observations on human nature, and his use of **dialect** have secured Clemens's place among great American writers.

GEORGE WASHINGTON CARVER (c. 1861–1943)

Born into slavery near Diamond Grove, George Washington Carver became the director of agricultural research at Tuskegee Institute in 1896. There he developed a variety of products from peanuts and sweet potatoes. Carter's work helped convince southern farmers that it was profitable to grow crops other than cotton.

SCOTT JOPLIN (1868–1917)

Scott Joplin is known as the "King of **Ragtime**." He settled in Missouri in 1895. His classic piano rags, such as "The Entertainer" and "The Maple Leaf Rag," had an important impact on the birth of jazz. Interest in Joplin's music revived in the 1970s when it was used in the award-winning score of the film *The Sting*.

HARRY S. TRUMAN (1884–1972)

Born in Lamar, Harry Truman became the vice president of the United States in 1944. When President Franklin D. Roosevelt died, Truman became the 33rd president of the United States. He led the country through the end of World War II and the early years of the Cold War. He is remembered for his ability to make tough decisions.

I DIDN'T KNOW THAT!

James Cash Penney (1875–1971) was born in Hamilton. He launched his first retail store in 1907 and built a chain of hundreds of stores. He included all employees in the chain's profit-sharing plan, which was unusual at the time. Today, there are more than 1,100 JCPenney stores throughout the United States and Puerto Rico. JCPenney is one of the largest retail chains in the country.

Maya Angelou (1928–) was born in St. Louis and became a writer in the 1950s. She is best known for her poetry and autobiographies that explore the themes of race, womanhood, and economic inequality.

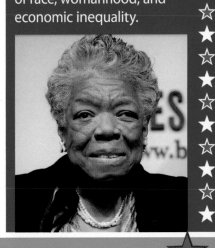

Population

With a population of almost 6 million in the 2010 Census, Missouri ranked 18th among the states. Its growth rate of 7 percent between 2000 and 2010 was below the average for all states. If the population were evenly spread across Missouri, there would be about 87 people on every square mile of land. Due to the rugged **terrain**, the Ozark region is less populous than the rest of state.

Kansas City is Missouri's largest city by population, but if suburbs are included, the St. Louis metropolitan area is larger. Some of Kansas City's suburbs are in Kansas, and the St. Louis area extends across the Mississippi River into Illinois. Springfield, Independence, and Columbia are the other cities in the state with more than 100,000 people. With a population of slightly more than 40,000, Jefferson City is a small state capital.

Missouri Population 1950–2010

Missouri's population has grown steadily but slowly since the middle of the 20th century. What are some possible reasons why the population has not grown more quickly?

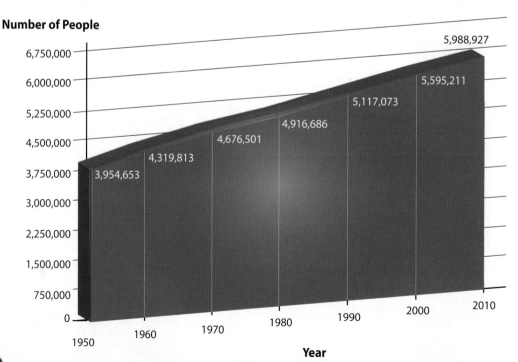

Number of People

Year	Number of People
1950	3,954,653
1960	4,319,813
1970	4,676,501
1980	4,916,686
1990	5,117,073
2000	5,595,211
2010	5,988,927

Year

Almost one-fourth of the people in Missouri are under the age of 18.

Missouri is home to more than 20 European cultural groups.

More than one-fourth of all Missourians claim to be of German ancestry.

African Americans make up more than 11 percent of the state's population. A large proportion of the African American population lives in the Kansas City and St. Louis areas. More than 30 percent of the people living in Kansas City, and more than half of the people in St. Louis, are African American.

With a population of almost 500,000, Kansas City is the largest city in Missouri. It covers parts of Jackson, Clay, Platte, and Cass counties. The Broadway Bridge crosses over the Missouri River into downtown Kansas City. To its west lies Kansas City, Kansas.

Politics and Government

Missouri has had four constitutions since joining the Union in 1821. The present constitution took effect in 1945. All **amendments** to the constitution must first be approved by a majority of voters. Like the federal government, there are three branches of government in Missouri. They are the executive, the legislative, and the judicial.

Missouri voters elect two U.S. senators. Starting in 2013, Missouri will have eight members in the U.S. House of Representatives. Because its population did not grow as much as some other states between 2000 and 2010, Missouri lost one seat in the House of Representatives as a result of the 2010 Census.

The beautiful State Capitol in Jefferson City was completed in 1917. The exterior is made of Missouri limestone marble.

The Missouri legislature works to fill the needs of the state. It recently passed a law helping Missouri's public colleges and universities to train more health care professionals.

Governors serve four-year terms. If elected to two terms in a row, a governor must step down at the end of the second term. The Missouri House of Representatives has 163 members, and the Senate has 34 members. These two chambers make up the state's General Assembly, or legislature, which makes new laws. The Supreme Court of Missouri is the highest court in the state.

Cities and counties play an important role in state politics. Missouri was the first state in the country to allow its cities to have their own home rule **charters**. There are 114 counties in the state, plus St. Louis, which has the status of an independent city.

Missouri's state song is called the "Missouri Waltz."

Here is an excerpt from the song:

Hush-a-bye, ma baby,
    slumbertime is comin' soon;
Rest yo' head upon my breast
    while Mommy hums a tune;
The sandman is callin' where
    shadows are fallin',
While the soft breezes sigh as
    in days long gone by.

Way down in Missouri where
    I heard this melody,
When I was a little child upon
    my Mommy's knee;
The old folks were hummin';
    their banjos were strummin';
So sweet and low.

Strum, strum, strum,
    strum, strum,
Seems I hear those banjos
    playin' once again,
Hum, hum, hum, hum, hum,
That same old plaintive strain.

Cultural Groups

Missouri's rich heritage provides for a wealth of cultural activity. The Ozark region has a strong folk story tradition. Folk tales are told to large gatherings of eager listeners. Folk music, dancing, food, and crafts are also celebrated in festivals around the state. Homemade funnel cakes are a popular folk snack. Square dancing and clog dancing are performed while musicians play folk instruments. Fiddles, banjos, harmonicas, spoons, and mouth bows combine to create the traditional sounds of folk music. Many groups play a style of music called **bluegrass**.

European settlers brought their own traditions to Missouri. The large German American population hosts festivals, such as Oktoberfest in the fall. Bratwurst sausage, sauerkraut, and delicate strudel pastries are served. Missourians dance the German polka to music of the accordion and autoharp, a stringed instrument. Missouri also has many people of Irish, English, Polish, Greek, and Italian descent.

Many cities in Missouri, including St. Louis, St. Charles, and Hermann, celebrate the German festival Oktoberfest. In Hermann, Oktoberfest is celebrated every weekend in October.

Although many American Indians were driven out of Missouri by European settlement, today about 30,000 American Indians live in Missouri. American Indians honor their traditions at various celebrations. Performers gather around a traditional drum, beating a rhythm. They chant and sing the songs of their ancestors, often wearing traditional clothing and jewelry.

Missouri's rich African American culture is on display in Kansas City in the historic 18th and Vine area. During the early 1900s, this African American neighborhood produced some of the finest jazz ever recorded. Artists such as Count Basie, John Coltrane, and Charlie Parker have helped to make 18th and Vine a location that is known around the world.

In recent years the Hispanic and Asian populations of Missouri have been growing. Most members of these groups live in and around Missouri's large cities.

African Americans in Missouri celebrate their heritage in many ways, including joining in parades on Martin Luther King Day. The Martin Luther King Day celebration at Harris-Stowe University in St. Louis is the second-largest such celebration in the country.

I DIDN'T KNOW THAT!

Max Hunter, a traveling salesman from Missouri, recorded about 1,600 folk songs from the Ozark Mountains between 1956 and 1976.

In October of each year, Hannibal hosts the Autumn Historic Folklife Festival, where artisans demonstrate crafts from the mid-1800s.

Missouri has several communities of Amish, the "plain people" who traditionally live and farm without using such modern technology as electricity and gasoline-powered vehicles.

Independence is considered an important city by the Church of Jesus Christ of Latter-day Saints, or Mormons. The Mormons were forced out of Missouri in the 1830s in what became known as the Mormon War.

Missourians enjoy re-enacting and viewing the re-enactment of the Lewis and Clark Expedition's departure from St. Charles on the Missouri River in 1804.

Arts and Entertainment

As jazz music made its way up the Mississippi River from New Orleans, St. Louis became an important station along the way. Kansas City, however, is better known as a jazz center. Such greats as saxophonists Lester Young and Charlie Parker and bandleader Count Basie were part of the local scene. A little later St. Louis became a center for rhythm and blues, the place where Chuck Berry and Ike and Tina Turner made their reputations.

Missouri has produced many motion picture giants as well. Walt Disney grew up in Marceline and St. Louis. Director Robert Altman, known for such films as *M*A*S*H*, *Nashville*, and *The Player*, was born in Kansas City. Actors Jon Hamm, Kevin Kline, and Kathleen Turner all come from Missouri.

Quilting is a popular folk art in Missouri. The Missouri State Quilters Guild has more than 100 local clubs across the state. The guild holds an annual quilt show as well as other, local shows throughout the year.

Missouri has produced many talented writers. The poets T. S. Eliot, Langston Hughes, and Sara Teasdale were all born in Missouri. Eliot is considered one of the greatest poets of the 20th century, and most people think he had the Mississippi in mind when he wrote in a poem that "the river is a strong brown god." Laura Ingalls Wilder also lived in Missouri. She wrote many of the popular Little House series of books at her family home in the Ozarks.

In recent years the Ozark Mountain town of Branson has become a major center for live entertainment. More than 40 theaters offer a wide variety of shows, mostly musicals, performed by well-known entertainers.

Brad Pitt grew up in Springfield and attended the University of Missouri. In 1995 he was nominated for an Academy Award for Best Supporting Actor for his work in 12 Monkeys. In 2006 he was nominated for a Golden Globe Award for Best Supporting Actor for his work in Babel. Offscreen, Pitt is known for his humanitarian efforts in New Orleans, Haiti, and other areas where disaster has struck.

I DIDN'T KNOW THAT!

Scott Joplin's "Maple Leaf Rag" is said to have been the first piece of sheet music to sell 1 million copies.

Comedians John Goodman and Dick Gregory and television broadcaster Walter Cronkite all come from Missouri.

Missouri's French heritage comes to life in many state events. Bastille Days and *Fête d'Automne* are two festivals where French food and entertainment are celebrated.

The Missouri Historical Society displays items relating to the famous *Spirit of St. Louis*, an airplane that was named in honor of the St. Louisans who paid for it. Pilot Charles Lindbergh used this plane to make the historic first solo flight across the Atlantic Ocean in 1927.

The singer and dancer Josephine Baker was born in St. Louis. Baker is known for taking African American jazz and culture to Paris in the 1920s.

Sports

Missourians, young and old, love sports. The state has a total of five major league sports teams. Baseball enthusiasts follow the St. Louis Cardinals and the Kansas City Royals. The St. Louis Rams and the Kansas City Chiefs play in the National Football League. In winter the St. Louis Blues hockey team hits the ice. This team was named in honor of a musical composition by W. C. Handy.

Missouri is also the site of several sports museums. In 1991 the Negro Leagues Baseball Museum opened in Kansas City. The museum celebrates the history of African American baseball. St. Louis, the home of several bowling champions, houses the International Bowling Museum & Hall of Fame. The Missouri Sports Hall of Fame is in Springfield.

Born in Jefferson City, Christian Cantwell was a track and field athlete at the University of Missouri. He is a three-time World Indoor Champion in the shot put and the 2009 World Outdoor Champion. Cantwell won the silver medal in the shot put at the 2008 Olympics.

Many Missourians enjoy canoeing on Table Rock or Clearwater lake. They also like to canoe on rivers such as the Current, Jacks Fork, or Niangua.

Outdoor sports are popular in Missouri. The state's rivers are ideal for canoeing and rafting, and cyclists can cover the 200-mile-long Katy Trail. With more than 6,300 caves in the state, **spelunking** is another favorite activity. Some of the more popular caves include Meramec Caverns, hideout of the outlaw Jesse James, and the Mark Twain Cave near Hannibal, where a famous episode in *Adventures of Tom Sawyer* is set.

Fishing and hunting are common pursuits in Missouri's many lakes, rivers, and forests. Game hunters seek out quail, pheasant, wild turkey, rabbit, and deer. Fishers catch bass, catfish, bluegill, and jack salmon. Float fishing is common in the Ozarks. Float fishers travel down rivers and around lakes, trailing fishing line behind them.

National Averages Comparison

The United States is a federal republic, consisting of fifty states and the District of Columbia. Alaska and Hawai'i are the only non-contiguous, or non-touching, states in the nation. Today, the United States of America is the third-largest country in the world in population. The United States Census Bureau takes a census, or count of all the people, every ten years. It also regularly collects other kinds of data about the population and the economy. How does Missouri compare to the national average?

Comparison Chart

United States 2010 Census Data *	USA	Missouri
Admission to Union	NA	August 10, 1821
Land Area (in square miles)	3,537,438.44	68,885.93
Population Total	308,745,538	5,988,927
Population Density (people per square mile)	87.28	86.94
Population Percentage Change (April 1, 2000, to April 1, 2010)	9.7%	7.0%
White Persons (percent)	72.4%	82.8%
Black Persons (percent)	12.6%	11.6%
American Indian and Alaska Native Persons (percent)	0.9%	0.5%
Asian Persons (percent)	4.8%	1.6%
Native Hawaiian and Other Pacific Islander Persons (percent)	0.2%	0.1%
Some Other Race (percent)	6.2%	1.3%
Persons Reporting Two or More Races (percent)	2.9%	2.1%
Persons of Hispanic or Latino Origin (percent)	16.3%	3.5%
Not of Hispanic or Latino Origin (percent)	83.7%	96.5%
Median Household Income	$52,029	$46,847
Percentage of People Age 25 or Over Who Have Graduated from High School	80.4%	81.3%

*All figures are based on the 2010 United States Census, with the exception of the last two items.

How to Improve My Community

S trong communities make strong states. Think about what features are important in your community. What do you value? Education? Health? Forests? Safety? Beautiful spaces? Government works to help citizens create ideal living conditions that are fair to all by providing services in communities. Consider what changes you could make in your community. How would they improve your state as a whole? Using this concept web as a guide, write a report that outlines the features you think are most important in your community and what improvements could be made. A strong state needs strong communities.

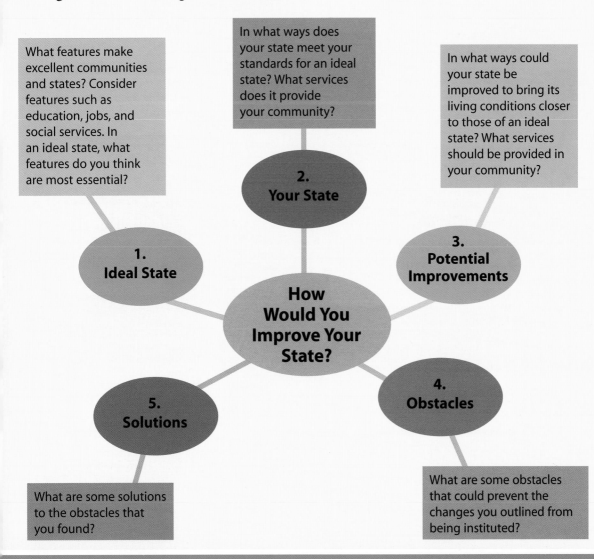

What features make excellent communities and states? Consider features such as education, jobs, and social services. In an ideal state, what features do you think are most essential?

In what ways does your state meet your standards for an ideal state? What services does it provide your community?

In what ways could your state be improved to bring its living conditions closer to those of an ideal state? What services should be provided in your community?

2.
Your State

1.
Ideal State

3.
Potential Improvements

How Would You Improve Your State?

5.
Solutions

4.
Obstacles

What are some solutions to the obstacles that you found?

What are some obstacles that could prevent the changes you outlined from being instituted?

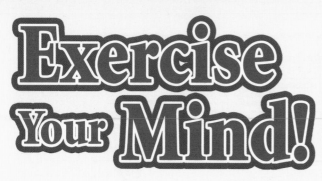

Exercise Your Mind!

Think about these questions and then use your research skills to find the answers and learn more fascinating facts about Missouri. A teacher, librarian, or parent may be able to help you locate the best sources to use in your research.

1 Which well-known animator opened his first studio in Kansas City?

2 What was Mark Twain's real name?

3 Where was the first kindergarten in the United States established?

4 Which native Missourian once lived in the White House?

5 Which foods may have been invented at the World's Fair in St. Louis in 1904?

6 What was the Missouri Compromise?

7 Which Missouri city is known for its many boulevards and fountains?

8 Which well-known scientist was born near Diamond Grove?

Words to Know

amendments: changes to a law or constitution

bluegrass: a style of hard-driving country music featuring the banjo

charters: documents that set out the rights of an organization or a group

Confederacy: the Southern states that opposed the Union in the Civil War

confluence: the place where two or more rivers join

dialect: speech that is characteristic of a certain region

drainage basin: the area drained by a river

ecosystems: all the elements of an environment and how they interact

extinction: no longer living on Earth

fertile: rich in the nutrients required to grow crops

free states: states that did not permit slavery

geodesic dome: a light dome structure made out of interlocking surfaces

ragtime: a type of music played mainly on the piano, developed out of African American folk music

reservations: lands reserved for American Indians

reservoir: artificially created body of water

segregation: forced separation and restrictions based on race

slave states: states that permitted slavery

spelunking: exploring caves and underground caverns

terrain: land

Index

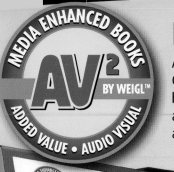

Log on to www.av2books.com

AV² by Weigl brings you media enhanced books that support active learning. Go to www.av2books.com, and enter the special code found on page 2 of this book. You will gain access to enriched and enhanced content that supplements and complements this book. Content includes video, audio, web links, quizzes, a slide show, and activities.

Audio
Listen to sections of the book read aloud.

Video
Watch informative video clips.

Embedded Weblinks
Gain additional information for research.

Try This!
Complete activities and hands-on experiments.

WHAT'S ONLINE?

 Try This!

Test your knowledge of the state in a mapping activity.

Find out more about precipitation in your city.

Plan what attractions you would like to visit in the state.

Learn more about the early natural resources of the state.

Write a biography about a notable resident of Missouri.

Complete an educational census activity.

 Embedded Weblinks

Discover more attractions in Missouri.

Learn more about the history of the state.

Learn the full lyrics of the state song.

 Video

Watch a video introduction to Missouri.

Watch a video about the features of the state.

EXTRA FEATURES

Audio
Listen to sections of the book read aloud.

Key Words
Study vocabulary, and complete a matching word activity.

Slide Show
View images and captio and prepare a presenta

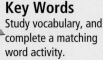

Quizzes
Test your knowledge.

AV² was built to bridge the gap between print and digital. We encourage you to tell us what you like and what you want to see in the future.

Sign up to be an AV² Ambassador at www.av2books.com/ambassador.